Prayers of an Omega

Prayers of an Omega

Facing
the Transitions
of Aging

Katie Funk Wiebe

HERALD PRESS
Scottdale, Pennsylvania
Waterloo, Ontario

Library of Congress Cataloging-in-Publication Data
Wiebe, Katie Funk.
    Prayers of an omega / Katie Funk Wiebe.
    p. cm.
    ISBN 0-8361-3658-6 (alk. paper)
    1. Aging—Religious aspects—Christianity. 2. Aged—Prayer-
books and devotions—English. 3. Wiebe, Katie Funk. I. Title.
BV4580.W48   1944
248.8'5—dc20   93-43266
                                                         CIP

The paper used in this publication is recycled and meets the
minimum requirements of American National Standard for Informa-
tion Sciences—Permanence of Paper for Printed Library Materials,
ANSI Z39.48-1984.

PRAYERS OF AN OMEGA
Copyright © 1994 by Herald Press, Scottdale, Pa. 15683
    Published simultaneously in Canada by Herald Press,
    Waterloo, Ont. N2L 6H7. All rights reserved
Library of Congress Catalog Number: 93-43266
International Standard Book Number: 0-8361-3658-6
Printed in the United States of America
Book design by Gwen M. Stamm
Cover art and design by Ingrid Hess

1 2 3 4 5 6 7 8 9 10 00 99 98 97 96 95 94

Dedicated to my mother
Anna Janzen Funk
for her steadfast faith

Contents

To pray these prayers

For a dozen or more years I have listened to older adults discuss what it means to grow older. Sometimes they drop just a small phrase giving me a clue to their real feelings about traversing the territory called "old age."

Older adults often speak freely when full of praise and joy. But feelings of uncertainty, vulnerability, loneliness, and powerlessness are also very much part of their lives. These feelings are often omitted in the public and sometimes even private prayers of older adults. Sometimes this is only because words to phrase these difficult feelings are hard to find.

With this book I hope to offer the gift of speech to older adults who feel inadequate to speak to God for and about themselves in a challenging situation. I have tried to incorporate a wide variety of experiences and feelings into these prayers. My aim in these contemporary psalms and prayers has been to be as open as the psalmists who poured out their feelings about the enemy facing them or the God who had delivered them.

Sometimes I have used the literary pattern of the Old Testament lament and praise psalms. Other times the prayer is an intimate conversation with God about what is happening in the speaker's life. To meet God at every step of life's journey is most important.

Older adults will soon be the largest demographic group in society as well as in the church. These prayers do not deny the realities of growing older. But they assert that the older person is someone God loves. Older Christians continue to be disciples of Christ and members of the church (even if absent from it). These prayers are rooted in the conviction that the inner life can grow even as the physical body weakens.

I have grouped the prayers in five untitled divisions. The first deals with the transition into the land of the older adult, the second with family life, the third with specific changes an older adult faces (like moving to a nursing home), and the fourth with the trials that challenge faith (like illness, loneliness, and death). The last group deals with the older adult's acceptance of mortality in light of the reality of death and the task of handing over the work of the kingdom to the next generation.

Some readers will read the book straight through as they would any book. Some will turn to the prayers that come closest to their interest and experience. And others will use the prayers as part of daily devotional reading.

The prayers show faith at work and offer an opportunity to correct attitudes. May these prayers also open the way to better listening on the part of readers who live close to these Omegas—meaning the last in the series.

I thank Ronald D. Guengerich, pastor of Whitestone Mennonite Church, Hesston, Kansas, for first showing me the importance of writing my own psalm-prayers. I am indebted to Tabor College student Bill Bush, who introduced me to the term "humpday" in one of his psalms written from the perspective of a student. I value the sensitive suggestions for revision offered by my daughter Christine Wiebe. I also thank all adults older than I am for their testimonies of faith, which have strengthened me in my pilgrimage. They are my cloud of fire by day and pillar of light by night.

—Katie Funk Wiebe
Wichita, Kansas

I

Now I am
an Omega

Though my father and my mother forsake me,
the Lord will receive me. (Ps. 27:10)

God, my everlasting Comforter, we buried Mom today.
We laid her in the ground, next to Dad. Now I am an
Omega, the last in our family. I've moved to the head of
the line.

Now the storms of life can beat directly upon me. No
buffer. I used to think of Mother as an umbrella, holding
God's love over us like a shield. She prayed every day for
each of us by name—children, grandchildren, and great-
grandchildren. She used to say that was how she remembered the names.

Now no one covers all of us with her prayers. I stand
alone to pray for my children and myself. And sometimes
I forget. My umbrella is gone. And it's cold and wet in the
rain.

Lord, I'm probably next in line to die. The generation

above me is all gone. Now I have to be strong for the generation below me. My children. Their children. And I don't feel able. I'm not ready to be patient, long-suffering, and forgiving as Mother was.

And I'm afraid of the darkening shadows. Of being an Omega. It was easier being an Alpha, a child, near the beginning.

Driving home late at night, we children slumped together in the backseat of the car like four loosely packed sacks of potatoes. Though it was dark and the road was bumpy, we knew we were going to that wonderful place called home. Dad was driving. Mother was watching. We knew we were safe. We would get there.

Mother and Dad did the best they could to raise us with what understandings of family relationships they had. And daily trusted in God's grace. They worked out understandings with their own past. And worked hard at bringing us up. And kept on praying and loving.

Now Mother and Dad are both gone. I am an Omega, the last in a series. And I am afraid.

Yet you, Lord, promise to carry us like a mother eagle that spreads her wings beneath the unsure eaglet testing its flying strength. You promise to bear us should we fall.

So, Lord, spread your strong arms of love around me and steady my faltering feet. Let me travel hopefully. Carry me, an Omega, by your grace. Lord, I trust you. Amen.

The law of old age

*Though outwardly we are wasting away, yet
inwardly we are being renewed day by day.*
(2 Cor. 4:16)

Lord God, I'm troubled this evening. I told her I was old,
which upset her. She said I was never to say that bad
word again.

Why not, Lord? To admit to being old, she said, was to
shift to "an unhealthy holding pattern for death." It
meant I was waiting to slide into the finish line. That's no
good, she said. You are getting older, but you're never
old.

Never old, Lord?

To her an old person means someone you're
ashamed of, someone who wears mismatched, washed-
out clothes, and parades stains on the front of a blouse or
shirt. Being old means becoming a boring fool who hol-
lers, "Whaddya say?" She thinks it means checking out of
the world before you're done with it.

God of all ages, I am puzzled. Am I old or am I not

old? When am I old? Is old age something to deny to the last breath as if it represents your wrath? Why shouldn't I say I am old?

God, you who promised to be with me to my last breath, what disturbs me? What have I missed? What has she missed?

Can I be your disciple when I am old—or only if I deny being old?

Faith without works is dead, wrote the apostle James. Where are the works of old age when I can no longer move about easily and volunteer for projects?

I think there's a law of old age that's as certain as the law of gravity. Being old means both letting go and yet hanging on. It means longing to be with you in glory and yet wanting to be here with the children. It means knowing life is ending but accepting each day as a new opportunity for your grace. It doesn't mean releasing the brakes while pressing the accelerator to the floor.

Give me grace to probe this—your law—and make it the rule of my life. Amen.

Yes, I am old!

*Trust in the Lord with all your heart and lean
not on your own understanding; in all your
ways acknowledge him, and he will make
your paths straight.* (Prov. 3:5-6)

Eternal Watcher of the young and old, today I see more
clearly. Today I declare boldly: old age can have its new
day as much as youth. Let the law of old age—yielding
and reaching—be evident in my life.

Help me to let go of the carefree independence of
youth and accept with grace and dignity increasing de-
pendence on others.

Give me courage to yield to the limitations of my
body but also boldness to explore the far reaches of the
mind and spirit. Though my body keeps moving into a
smaller and smaller world, keep my mind and spirit strid-
ing into the kingdom of your Spirit.

Though my feet move more unsteadily, my eyes see
less clearly, and my ears hear less distinctly, may I walk
more surely in your ways. May I see in vivid colors the

richness of your love for me, and may I hear clearly even the faintest whispers of your encouragement.

Free me from a sense of powerlessness and worthlessness. Open my mind to accept the invitation of creativity. Though my body may be diminishing, my spirit can soar. When that happens, I can say boldly, "I am old."

Let this time of being old be a time to trust, not to doubt, a time to be gentle, not to stand in judgment, a time to walk unhurriedly, for God doesn't depend on me to save the world or even to run it.

Let me bring understanding and humor into any room, so people see in me the freedom of laughter.

Keep me from self-pity and grumpiness. My tongue speaks too quickly of my aches and pains. Instead make me willing to listen to the pain of others.

Let me see that the real stains are not food drips on my clothes but bitterness, criticism, and gossip that make an indelible mark on the spirit.

Lord, teach me that this is not the time to clutch my possessions to myself but to let go of my attachment to everything made of wood, cloth, metal, paper, and plastic. Give me grace to relinquish the pleasure of power and to hand the controls over to the next generation.

To make more room for you, root from my heart all things that uselessly take up space. May I never let go of a passion for love, truth, honesty, justice, joy, beauty, peace. When death comes, may it be a stepping lightly over the threshold into the new life, unburdened by heavy thoughts of possessions.

Above all, Lord God, let me be the bearer of this news

to those younger than I: being old means always moving toward the goal of maturity in Christ Jesus, not standing still. Old age is that great and glorious promised land where faith is fulfilled.

God is good!

*Every good and perfect gift is from above, com-
ing down from the Father of the heavenly lights,
who does not change like shifting shadows.*
(James 1:17)

God, you are good! After days of despair and loneliness,
a day comes when your presence bursts upon me like a
fresh-flowing waterfall. I see you all about me.
  Thank you for this morning's warm shower,
      for colorful easy-to-wash-and-wear clothes,
      for the paper carrier who places my paper on the
          porch so I don't have to walk out to pick it up,
      for the trash collectors—even the noisy ones in the
          early morning who disturb my sleep,
      for the service station operator who looks at my car
          when I hear safety pins jangling underneath,
      for the glorious yellow rosebud I just picked,
      for the fat worm lolling in the wet grass after
          the rain,
      for not having to go to work on a wet, blustery day,

for malls to walk in when the winds blow and the
    rains pour,
for young people who hold heavy doors so I can
    enter,
for children who greet me by name when they
    see me,
for thermostats that summon up heat like a genie
    in a lamp,
for mute buttons on the television remote control
    to shut out the advertising din,
for clean benches in parks to rest awhile,
for fat cats that warm my feet at night,
for the sassy bluejay that bosses the birdfeeder
    outside my window,
for a telephone close at hand to call my friend,
for a friend to call and to pray with,
for kind travelers who lift my suitcase into the bin
    on the plane,
for the smile from the young woman at the super-
    market checkout.

Thank you for helping me remember the hidden
place I put my wallet to keep it safe.

Thank you for people who ask me how I am and how
I slept and insist on helping me with my coat. The day
may come when no one will be interested in me.

Thank you that I don't want the many things for sale
at discount prices that I don't need.

Thank you for your Word of truth, which brings
strength and comfort.

Thank you for life, for love, for joy. Amen.

Bald heads and purple hair

*Are not five sparrows sold for two pennies? Yet
not one of them is forgotten by God. Indeed,
the very hairs of your head are all numbered.
Don't be afraid; you are worth more than
many sparrows.* (Luke 12:6-7)

Beautiful Savior, am I still beautiful? I have no one to ask
but you. Younger friends say with great enthusiasm,
"You're looking great for your age," but I'm not sure
what that means.

I look into the mirror and see deep lines tracing the
contours of my face. The veins on my arms and hands
stand out like thick ropes. My gnarled finger joints poke
out like burrs on a tree. My hair grows thinner every day.

I see the joggers float by my window and want to join
them but my body refuses. I weep for the old man dod-
dering along on the walking path in the sunshine. His
youth has fled—and mine is following his fast.

Lord God, I'm really asking two questions: should I let the hairdresser give me purple hair like Loretta's? Should I buy a new coat when the old one still fits and is not worn out?

The problem is that my coat is almost ancient and styled for the 1970s. Does old age deserve new clothes? Do older people need new things, though beauty of face and figure may be denied them?

I can't change the way I look.

I can't wear a mask to cover the brown spots.

But I can go a long way on a new smile meant just for me.

I can go longer on a kind word.

And even longer on a spontaneous word of affection. For that do I need a full head of dark hair, a new coat, and shining pumps?

You, Lord, look on the inside. You can count hairs on bald heads, blonde heads, brown heads, and purple heads. You don't care whether the coat is old and worn or new and stylish.

Children of God are always beautiful. Peace-loving people are always beautiful. The face of wisdom is always beautiful. Mature, serene people are always beautiful.

I think the young bride at the wedding last week was radiantly beautiful, yet her mother showed greater charm and grace despite her gray hair. And the wrinkled grandmother? Her face reflected the wisdom of years of experience. That was true beauty.

So I declare it boldly: I am a child of God. My body is the temple of the Holy Ghost. God loves me with gray hair, dark hair, or purple hair. Loretta with purple hair is beautiful and I with my white hair am also beautiful.

But it may be time for a new coat, even one with a red plaid lining.

Lord, I don't like lawn mowers

If that is how God clothes the grass of the field,
which is here today and tomorrow is thrown
into the fire, will he not much more clothe you,
O you of little faith? (Matt. 6:30)

Lord, I don't like lawn mowers. You're the only one I can say that to, so I'll say it again: I don't like lawn mowers.

I don't like the noise. They're like large bluebottle flies buzzing up and down the neighborhood.

I don't like the way the neighbors' lawn mowers produce neatly clipped lawns I must try to match.

I don't like the way lawn mowers overpopulate the neighborhood. Every neighbor has one and sometimes two or three, and they usually pollute the agreeable silence on Sunday afternoon when we're visiting on the patio.

I don't like them when the blades get dull, when the underside clogs up, when the bag fills up in one round, and especially when I pull my arms out of their sockets trying to get them started.

I don't like the way they try my patience, my endurance, my appreciation for carefully groomed lawns.

Paul had a thorn in the flesh that wouldn't go away. A lawn mower isn't a thorn in the flesh, only a teensy splinter.

Would you ever have said, "Consider the lawn mowers on the lawn. They toil but they do not reap"?

Or "Come unto me, all ye that labor at lawn mowing and are heavy laden"?

If you had lived today, would your yard have looked as neat as that of the others in your Nazareth neighborhood? Would you have put a stumbling block in your neighbor's way by letting your grass grow tall and rank? Were they invented to teach us patience?

I get it. You are living today—in me. And I have to decide to do this job with joy or reject it as your plan.

I really don't know. Maybe more ornamental rock is the answer. I commit to you all lawn mowers of the world. And their keepers. And pray for grace and wisdom.

This old dog learned a new trick today

Blessed is he whose transgressions are forgiven,
whose sins are covered. (Ps. 32:1)

I come before you, almighty God, Redeemer, forgiver of sins, with my tail between my legs. Today you taught this old dog a new trick. Not that you didn't try to teach me this before, but I never caught on. You spoke to me about it again and again, but I didn't want to learn.

I was a believer in Christ. I knew and cherished your forgiveness of my sins. But I couldn't forgive her for what she had done to me. And I never saw my hardness as sin.

Today I learned that an older person like myself can forgive someone even for something that happened long ago but left a bad and lingering memory. The hurt happened unexpectedly—she made fun of the way I talked in front of my friends. She ridiculed me—and I could never forget. Every time I thought of her, my hurt leaped onto my back like an angry cat I couldn't shake off.

I often thought about what I would like to say to her if I ever got her alone. In the night hours when I couldn't sleep, I prepared long speeches that would make her sit back and recognize her offense.

Other times I dismissed it. Just a problem in personal relationships, I told myself. Stay apart. But this robbed me of the opportunity to know her better and to benefit from her friendship.

Yet, Lord, I told you often she had no right to speak of me in that way, especially before my friends. She had made me like a piece of garbage thrown into the gutter.

I tried to numb myself to the pain. But it was no use.

I lost the joy of fellowship with you because her face always stood between you and me. I became bitter and watchful of her and of others. I wanted her to admit her guilt. Then I'd forgive her.

Then you showed me through your Word that you set up no preconditions for forgiving. The father forgave the prodigal son even before he returned.

You showed me that my pain, my unforgiving spirit, was my problem, not hers. As long as I couldn't forgive her, I was bound to her. The chains would become tighter and more painful with the passing years.

So your word was "Forgive as I forgive. Seventy times seven. Release her. Don't bind her to you with your anger." You said, "In faith, reach out and forgive. Let Christ's work on the cross give you the power to do so."

And I did. I could say, "I forgive you, friend. I know you in your weakness and your strength. I see you as a person made in the image of God. I see you as a person who also needs the love of Christ. I know you and I love you."

With those words, I was free. Free of my burden. She and I could start again. It didn't matter if she felt guilty about her idle words. That was her problem with you. She may hurt me again, and I may have to forgive her again. But the slate has been cleared.

You have released me from the past, healed the present, and made the future a possibility of joy. I praise your matchless name. Amen.

Wise words
for old-agers

Wisdom calls aloud in the street, she raises her voice in the public squares; at the head of the noisy streets she cries out, in the gateways of the city she makes her speech. (Prov. 1:20-21)

God of all wisdom and truth, I've no pulpit to preach from, but I have a speech to make about what I've learned on the way to becoming older.

Welcome each day with anticipation of what God has in store for you. Close it off with thanksgiving.

Sing in the shower, dance in the kitchen, jog in the park, whistle while you wait.

Visit with the postman, the nurse in the doctor's office, the man at the service station, the woman sitting next to you at a lecture. Talk about the weather, your rose bushes, about the dog next door—anything except your own aches and pains, operations and treatments, intake of calories and cholesterol, sleep and bathroom habits.

If your husband asks you to walk around the block with him once, go with him twice.

Feed the birds and starve the mice.

Pick the flowers in your own garden; pick up empty pop cans in the park.

Treat your corns and bunions with a trip to a podiatrist. Treat yourself with a trip to the library.

Never hand someone a dead fish. Shake hands as if you meant it.

Don't slobber kisses on anyone over the age of six.

Organize your spices; let your books and magazines mess up the place.

Take an escalator to the second floor and the stairs down.

Before you phone a friend long distance, turn the clock around. Skimp on butter and margarine, lavish friendship and kindness.

Make up a ridiculous name when you meet someone you know but whose name you have forgotten, and you'll keep your friend.

Buy a whole sheet of stamps at a time and see how fast you can use them on friends and family.

The person who is a profligate with compliments and stingy with criticism will never want a friend.

When you can't remember where you placed something for safekeeping, forget you owned it. When you find it, you'll be the first to be surprised.

There are three things that are never satisfied, four that never say, "Enough!": the clock that runs on batteries, the popcorn popper, the houseplants by a south window, and the grandchild who likes homemade stories.

The homemaker who throws out or gives away at least one or two items for every knickknack, doodad, gadget, and item of clothing she brings into the house will always have a place to set a cup of coffee for a friend and grateful children when she leaves this world.

Grandparents who give their grandsons and grand-daughters standing ovations at every game or other performance they take part in will never be forgotten.

If your fat friend asks you to join her for a piece of apple pie, suggest an apple instead. If the invitation comes from your skinny friend, recommend it be served a la mode. The wise person makes the friend's needs her needs.

Be ready in five seconds whenever your son offers to go shopping for a new jacket for you. He may be hinting it's time for a change.

Better a meal of tofu and sprouts where there is love than roast beef and baked potatoes with sour cream and harsh words.

Like a beautiful Rembrandt hung in the chicken barn is the well-groomed, well-exercised elder who gripes all day long.

II

Homecoming

God sets the lonely in families. (Ps. 68:6)

Well, Father/Mother God, this is our time together again. And I'm tired. My feet feel as if they belong to someone else. They're numb and swollen from preparing food and making beds.

The children are all gone once again, back to their own places of belonging. Our good times are over for a while.

For a few days this old house was much too small—clothes, suitcases, damp towels, water glasses, and more were scattered over everything that doesn't move when touched. I heard the screen door opening and closing at least once every five minutes and the refrigerator door nearly as often.

But it was wonderful! And I thank you for it, Lord. Children are a special blessing. And grandchildren a double blessing.

The family was your idea, Lord. You set the lonely in families. You sent the sick man back to his family when he was healed. You took care of your own mother even when you were on the cross.

There is a purpose for the family that becomes clearer as I get older. When we're young we feel (rather than know) that a home is intended to be a haven, an oasis of peace to which each member can come after the day's turmoil. When young I knew that even if misunderstood or criticized by schoolmates, I'd be accepted at home.

The children are gone again. What did we try to teach the children all these years? Lesson plans—did we have any?

I hope they have learned that a home is place where parents know each child by name, and where each child's art work, writings, and pictures have a private showing regularly on the refrigerator door.

I hope they have learned that home is where there is always a spot for each child at the table and where each one knows that whatever food is available will be shared.

I hope they have learned that if they ever have to go home, we are ready to take them in, even if only into a single room and a bathroom down the hall.

I hope they have learned that a home is a place to live with hope, love, and forgiveness. I hope at home they have learned that we can make choices: to allow our lives to be shaped by the sin that is the lot of all humankind or to accept God's mercy. Neither we the parents nor they the children need stand condemned forever. There is always abundant grace.

I hope they have learned that a home is a place to create memories, both good and bad. And homecoming is a time to share these memories and laugh, without rancor, about mistakes and shortcomings.

When they were young we had no Walton family to use as a model for family harmony. But something special happens when children start telling their own stories about their childhood just as I and my siblings like to talk about our early days.

But now, Lord, the third cycle has started. The table keeps getting more crowded. The little ones remember, with the accuracy of a computer, where the toys are kept. The very smallest one can jump with two feet and say "shovel" clearly—although no one can think up a good reason why a two-year-old should say "shovel" on a Sunday afternoon. But this is family.

As I sit here and reminisce, I wonder, Lord, how the children saw us, their mother and father, as they were growing up. I always thought my parents were much too cautious. Only when my husband and I had to balance an unbalanceable budget did I understand my parents' reluctance to overspend.

Our children always went with us to Sunday school and church, to the homes of friends, and to concerts. Babysitters weren't part of our agenda in those days. And we always agreed jokingly before we left that if we didn't enjoy the company, one of us would furtively pinch the baby so we could go home.

Now they've gone home.

For a few days you gave us the privilege of enjoying one another.

The children found the old record of Dr. Seuss' *Yertle*

the Turtle. The record has been much abused and needs some coaxing. As the story unfolded, I noticed my own adult children reciting in unison with the narrator. When the record stuck, they feared they'd miss Gertrude McLeish's screech of dismay. But it was there. And they added to it their own cries of glee, though they are now parents themselves.

Memories like this make the ties that bind the family together stronger and more lasting than any other ties on earth. Thanks for this wonderful time with family members. May the circle be unbroken for a long time. Let there be a homecoming in eternity for us all.

On the birth
of a grandchild

"What then is this child going to be?"
(Luke 1:66)

I praise you this evening, Lord, with an overflowing heart. My grandson was born this morning. Perfect in every detail.

I stand in awe of the beauty of his small body. I am grateful for your goodness in giving them this much-wanted child, yet mindful of those parents whose child may have come into the world with a weakness, a handicap. Be with them in their pain. Comfort them in their sorrow. Give them courage to find the door to hope again.

This precious child's dark blue eyes look with wonder, seeing yet not seeing the brave new world beyond the darkness of the womb. He is already reaching out, eager to share our lives and learn about the adventure ahead.

What did Simeon and Anna see in the child Jesus when he came with his parents to the temple? What is this child going to be? I ask. What road do you have for him to follow?

Only yesterday our own youngsters were sitting around our table. We never questioned whether to have children. A family wasn't a family without children. We accepted each child, planned or unplanned, as God's gift.

Milk spills at breakfast and torn dresses after school brought their share of irritation. We paid for dentist bills and crayons, music lessons and sneakers. I made angel costumes for Christmas concerts and new dresses for Easter.

When the children were small, we staggered out of bed at night to bring them water and lead them to the bathroom. Later, when they were older, we waited bleary-eyed and heartsick into the dawn if the clock showed later than the agreed-upon time for arriving home. Only then did I understand why my parents worried about my late nights.

We were committed to childrearing because we had brought the children into the world. At bedtime we read to them from *Little Pilgrim's Progress* and *Grimm's Fairy Tales*. We loved and disciplined the children, scolded them and felt proud of them, argued with them and for them. And pushed them toward you. Sometimes too hard. Forgive me, Lord.

We shoved the children off to school with a sigh of relief, yet we were jealous of every new influence on their lives. We never reckoned fully with the tug on their spirits of friends and their music.

When the children came home with new ideas and words, we laughed at their newfound worldly wisdom—and sometimes cried. They were moving into young adulthood and away from us. We wanted them to grow up. Yet I wanted them to remain small, clinging to my skirts.

We trembled and cried when their decisions seemed to lead to self-defeat—and hollered hallelujah when they climbed mountains and walked on water. When their lives were filled with pain, we found we could not heal the disease or pull out the loneliness or disappointment like a weed. We could only point them to you, the healer of broken hearts and bodies.

Lord, why didn't we have a greater awareness of the need to develop strong self-images in our children? But then who worried about good self-images when we were children? Like Topsy we just grew.

Mother and Dad did the best they knew how. And trusted in God's grace. And prayed. And we did the best we knew how for our children—and now we agonize over whether we stroked too little or paddled too much. And pray for forgiveness.

Now another father and mother have a chance to show what love can do. I dedicate this new life to beauty, to truth, to love, and to joy.

Lord, be kind to this child. Show him mercy when he stumbles. Let him learn early about forgiveness and grace. Let him claim when he is still young his right to creativity. Let him not sell his birthright of freedom in

Christ for bondage to a mess of pottage.

May my love help make the ground steady under his feet and teach him confidence and joy. He is your child. I commit him to your keeping. Amen.

Running interference

Pray continually. (1 Thess. 5:17)

God, coach of my team, tonight I'm running interference. It's hard work. My feet are tired, my heart is pounding, and my breath comes short. It looks as if the offense is going to get the ball and run with it unless I help stop them. I want the children to win this game.

The children of this world seem much too young to do battle with what their eager eyes see, their open ears hear, their ready mouths taste, their inexperienced bodies feel, and their vulnerable minds are encouraged to imagine.

The bright promise of instant happiness, overpowering thrills, and quick money dances temptingly before them. The world invites them to become gluttons of its colorful display of experiences. It encourages them to waste their talents on selfish concerns.

Satan's got the ball and is running to the goal line with it. And he scores far too often. With the young girl who was bored with school and ran away from home. With the young boy who couldn't resist finding out what it felt like to be really high. With the college student who has decided that making more money than his father did is a significant goal.

And so I intercede for them, Giver of all good gifts. Cleanse their ambitions. Help them to learn to play the game of life well.

Remind them to put on the shoulder pads of faith and love before they leave for school each day. May the hope of salvation be their helmet to protect them in head-on crashes with the enemy.

May they remember their Creator in the days of their youth. May you become their coach and the owner of their team, guiding them through this difficult passage to the end zone. Let them not be afraid of hard work or failure.

Give me endurance to run interference for them daily. I am older. I am more experienced. I know the wiles of the enemy a little better. I've played the game of life much longer. Answer my prayer for these children.

In your holy name, Lord Jesus, I plead. Amen.

God leads his dear children along

Hear my prayer, O Lord; let my cry for help come to you. Do not hide your face from me when I am in distress. Turn your ear to me; when I call, answer me quickly. (Ps. 102:1-2)

Hear my prayer, O Lord. Don't turn your ear from me, for I need you.

I need your counsel, your comfort, your strength.

I feel so lost, so alone, so helpless to do anything.

The children will not be moving back to this area after all—after five years of going to school, they're moving East. I don't know why.

Am I the reason, because I balked at their going to school at times?

Are you the reason, Lord? Are you leading them in this new path?

The letter we received today is vague, rambling— "better opportunity," it said. "The Lord's leading . . ."

I wanted so much to have them close. I planned for this from the day they first moved away. I took it for granted. I'd see them often. The grandchildren would learn to know me. We'd have lots of good times together.

The years were lonely waiting for their return. Each day moves by on leaden feet. I wait for it to end. My throat aches from swallowing. My heart is heavy. I cannot eat. I cannot pray.

I lie awake listening for your voice. I become a bird alone on a housetop. I am like a child lost in the woods and no one has scattered crumbs to show me the way.

My friends will say, "You shouldn't have counted on their coming back into this area. Children today don't want to be tied to their parents."

I sit and cry. I'm not ready to find another way, for I've been waiting these five years for them to return, to be close. I am lonely for family, because the ranks of my own friends are thinning each year.

But you, Lord, are still my God. Your faithfulness is known by many generations of my family. When Mother left Europe after World War II, she said good-bye to her mother not knowing if she would see her again. She never did. But you gave her faith to trust and joy to live.

We are all your children, Lord. Let your name yet be glorified in our lives wherever we live. You remain the same; you are eternal. All things work together for good to them who love the Lord, and I trust you, Lord, to work this situation out as well for your greater glory.

A prayer
for our schools

Remember your Creator in the days of your youth. (Eccles. 12:1)

All morning I've watched the children of the neighborhood tripping or cycling along the road in front of the house. They're going back to school with book bags, lunch kits, new clothes, and monstrous athletic shoes.

I sense they're eager to meet their old friends and find out who their teachers are. I pray for them as the new school year begins. I hope their parents are praying for them also.

I bow before you, Lord God, Creator of the universe, to acknowledge you as the giver of all good things—of life and love, of truth and beauty, of knowledge and wisdom. I praise you as the Savior and Redeemer of our souls.

I commit these children to you as they begin this school year.

The times we live in are noisy ones. Our ears are deafened by thousands of voices calling us in different directions.

Lord, may these children take off their earphones long enough to hear the sound of your voice calling them to purposeful living, to righteous living, to living that glorifies your name. May your Holy Spirit guide and protect each one from sin and evil.

I pray that these children may have a desire to know you and your truth. May they get caught up in the pursuit of excellence—not only in academic studies but in righteous and holy living.

I pray for parents. Many of these parents are rich in this world's goods but poverty-stricken when it comes to time. Help them to take time for their children, so they're more than a voice on the telephone and answering machine or a note on the fridge door. Let them be encouragers, listeners, and inspirers of dreams in their children.

I pray for school leaders—for administrators, teachers, and parents—that they may have eyes open to your vision for becoming a whole person in Christ. Give them courage, wisdom, and insight as they lead. And let them overwhelm the children with joy and laughter and love.

I pray for aides and janitors. Sometimes even one small word from them, even a smile, may turn a lonely child into a trusting one.

Today is a new beginning for these children, whom we hold in trust for you. Keep me conscious of this trust, not just today but each day of this school year.

III

Moving day

By faith Abraham . . . obeyed and went, even though he did not know where he was going. (Heb. 11:8)

God of the journey of life, this evening I rest in the ark of your faithfulness. I face a hard task tomorrow. I am moving from this six-room home my husband and I lived in for forty years to a solitary room in the nursing home. Hold me steady, Lord, in these quiet moments I have chosen to spend with you.

Something in me cries out that old trees should not be transplanted. At my age I dread any change, especially this one. A family builds a home only to see a stranger live in it. We gather memories to see them dispersed for nickels and dimes at a garage sale.

That tablecloth with the blue flowers I always liked sold for $2, the old rocking chair with the chintz covering in which I nursed all four children for $5.

I can't sleep at night without the mantel clock chiming the time when I waken in the darkness, but they took it also. The children said, "No room, Mom. We'll get you a small clock with a lighted dial."

Every time the children came to see me in recent months they asked when I'd be ready to move. "It's time," the children said, "time to think of moving to something smaller." My name was on the client list and moving on up, although I wished it would slide to the bottom.

The children saw this old house deteriorating. "The repairs are getting to be too much for you," they said. I saw each room growing more beautiful with memories of good times.

They saw my flower garden becoming smaller each year. In my imagination I saw the daring daffodils and careful crocuses peep through the soil each spring, like young girls in their first spring dresses. I didn't need the actual flowers to remind me the season of new life had begun. My garden was always still there next to the house.

The children saw me stumble when I walked too fast to greet them. But I knew I wasn't fumbling in my love for them.

And so finally I said yes.

But, God of my life, this evening as I sit here for the last time, looking at my walls stripped bare of the pictures and the old rug with its familiar footpaths, I am homesick already. The massive oak furniture we bought forty-five years ago when we married had to be sold because it wouldn't fit into a small room. Only my much-used walnut dresser and arm chair go with me.

Will I ever see the sunshine greet me with the unin-hibited joy of a child again? Will I ever smell the fresh fra-grance of lilacs in spring again? Will I ever trample piles of crisp leaves in fall and chase the squirrel up the tree again? Or linger with the neighbor over the fence at mid-morning? That was always the best visiting.

The glory of the past must rest as I sort the confusion of the present.

I hope someone will love this old house as much as we loved it. I wanted to leave instructions for the upstairs bathroom showerhead that sometimes doesn't work quite right. Diddling with the lever keeps it flowing. But Jerry says, "Forget it. The new owners will know what to do." But will they? Why should they buy a new one when this one works if you know how?

This transition to the nursing home is the last big move of my earthly journey before that move to the room Jesus has prepared for me. Make me as homesick for heaven, Lord, as I know I will be for this place I am leav-ing. Make me more aware that death means coming close to the Giver of all love and to those who have gone before.

Tomorrow give me grace to accept the challenge of a life away from my stainless steel sink and almond-colored stove and fridge I was so pleased with twenty years ago. How will I deal with never making another meal? With the loss in status that comes with dependent old age?

Rock of ages, I have trusted you as the source of my life and inspiration when my life was going well. I want to affirm your love and faithfulness when I cannot understand the path before me. Teach me to sing the songs of Zion in a strange land.

Go before me and prepare room 201 at Riverside Homes. Though it may be small, it will always be large enough for you and me. Amen.

I sure liked
to drive my car

*There is a time for everything, and a season for
every activity under heaven.* (Eccles. 3:1)

Lord, this morning I turned in my license to drive. I put it
in an envelope and wrote a note saying I wasn't going to
drive any more. The kids patted me on the back and said,
"Great, Dad. Good decision. We're all for you." Then
they drove the car away.

I think I felt relieved. At ease.

No more worrying whether I'd make the left turn onto
the highway before another car zoomed by. No more
worrying whether I'd see the little girl on the bicycle behind me. No more worrying whether the elusive shadows at night were pedestrians enjoying the evening air.

But I miss the feel of a ring of hard keys in my pocket.
I reach for them, just to give them a caress. But they're
not there. I want to go out and start the car. For no reason. Then I remember. The car is gone. I will never back

it out of the garage onto the road again. I will never again experience the power of the engine with me at the wheel.

We always had a quiet life. Not much traveling. Others talked about Disneyland and Yosemite, but we liked it here. At home. We had a car to dash to the store to get milk for breakfast. To go to church. And to visit the children. And to check on the waving wheatfields in early summer with windows open. Slow, poky Sunday drivers, they called us. We didn't mind.

The children say they'll take me anywhere I need to go. Just phone and they'll come. But my longing to see that lilac tree welcome the spring disappears when I have to squeeze a passing look at it between a dentist's appointment and a quick trip to the post office to catch the last mail. Middle-aged children haven't got time for nature's all-out shout of welcome in spring just yet.

Lord, I desperately want to know whether the redbuds bloomed this spring on the street where we used to live. I want to know what color Jim and Helen painted their house. I want to spend the afternoon driving—for no reason.

Reach out your hand, my Lord, and place it here in the warm hollow of my hand where I used to hold the keys.

Wednesday is Humpday

What has been will be again, what has been done will be done again; there is nothing new under the sun. (Eccles. 1:9)

God of all eternity, I didn't need to look at the calendar to tell me it is Humpday. Monday and Tuesday move by on snail's feet. Usually there's little or no mail. People don't call.

Then comes Wednesday. It's like the hump on a camel. Crawl over it and you slide off the end. Until Wednesday comes I'm climbing toward the hump, waiting for the weekend, for when people have time to call, and for going to church and maybe going out to eat.

Something in me doesn't like the monotony of the sameness of Monday, Tuesday, Wednesday. . . .

Decades ago Monday was washday.

Tuesday was ironing day.

Wednesday was prayer-meeting day. And after that we knew Sunday was coming. We were over the hump once again.

Thursday and Friday had their special assignments like shopping and mending, but Saturday and Sunday were the big days. We cleaned and polished floors and furniture, shoes and pots and pans. We baked and cooked and invited—it was important to be with friends and loved ones on Sunday.

We never missed church for any reason.

We never mowed the grass on Sunday for any reason.

We never went shopping on Sunday for any reason.

Sunday was a holy day because we spent it with you and with loved ones.

But now there is a sameness to the days. Being old feels like every day is Monday or Tuesday. I'm always waiting for Humpday.

I don't want to wish my life away week by week. But couldn't there be a little more Sunday in Monday and Tuesday?

Saturday is Hymnday

*Sing and make music in your heart to the
Lord, always giving thanks to God the Father
for everything, in the name of our Lord Jesus
Christ.* (Eph. 5:19-20)

Lord of song, I woke this morning with joy in my heart,
for today is Saturday, and Saturday is Hymnday. This is
my comfort time, my time to sing my way through the old
hymnbook.

I don't want to forget the old hymns I learned as a
child, for then I'd be turning my back on our journey together. I'd forget some of your love toward me.

I need these old hymns like a traveler longs for water
in a dry and thirsty land. I will need them till I walk
through the valley of the shadow of death.

Lord, you know I don't like to complain, but I can't
get used to these new choruses we'll sing tomorrow in
church. I try to clap and sway, but this old body doesn't
work that way. So Saturday I sing the old songs. To myself
and to you.

They are a record of my pilgrimage with you these many decades. And this record of your faithfulness slips from me unless I go over it again and again.

"Sing them over again to me, wonderful words of life . . ." That was the first piece I learned to play on the piano. And when your Word became wonderful to me, I enjoyed the hymn even more.

I liked singing "Shall We Gather at the River?" because we actually gathered at the river for a baptismal service. Scores of your children celebrated the decision of young Christians to walk with you. And dozens of unbelievers from the community watched from a distance. Outdoor baptismal services had something to say for themselves.

Our first choir song at college was "Amazing grace, how sweet the sound that saved a wretch like me." From our director I learned to sing with meaning, not just to make sounds.

Each Sunday at the end of the service in the little white church, the congregation sang, "Take thou my hand, O Father, and lead thou me." This was more than a token song to end the service. It was a prayer asking you to go with each one of us in that congregation into the struggle of the week. Those were the Depression years. Not all of those people in their much-washed clothing were certain of enough food for the coming week. I never felt ready to leave until we had sung that song, even as today I don't feel ready for the coming week until I have prayed that song.

We used to sing "There Shall Be Showers of Blessings" with more gusto than an overflow crowd at a close basketball game. But we dragged through forty-seven verses of "Just As I Am Without One Plea," waiting for someone to heed the minister's call. Sometimes I felt like walking to the altar to make him feel better. But there was another time, another place, when I did come to you without one plea. That song reminds me of that coming and of our beginning life together.

"Great Is Thy Faithfulness" and "How Great Thou Art" bring tears to my eyes whenever I hear them. When it seemed everyone had deserted me, you, Lord, remained close. You gave strength to turn the valley of Baca into a well of life.

The "thee's" and "thou's" and other old-fashioned words that upset some people don't bother me because I know you, the Giver of those words.

When I've sung the old hymns once again, my soul is at rest. They place my feet firmly in your truth. Thank you for songs of faith that speak the language of my soul. Now I'm ready for tomorrow, for the tumbling music of the praise choruses, and for all the rest.

Maybe, just maybe, when this generation is as old as I am, they'll have their own Saturday Hymnday. I'm betting on it, Lord.

Lament for
an unrecognized gift

*Trust in the Lord with all your heart and lean
not on your own understanding; in all your
ways acknowledge him, and he will make
your paths straight.* (Prov. 3:5)

Rescue me, Lord, for I am in despair. I feel it isn't worth
studying the Bible as diligently as I once did. Yet when
I'm not studying the Scriptures, you seem far away.

I am worn out trying to figure out how to get the
church to understand that I want to keep serving you the
same way I did as a missionary. But it's no use.

The church in my homeland doesn't recognize my
gifts of teaching and preaching. It's as if they don't know
my gifts once existed or that they remain as much a part
of me as my hands and feet. All they want is missionary
reports, not what we taught in the country that made
these reports about new believers possible.

Does that mean that you also don't see my continuing

Bible study as worthwhile? If you did value my Bible study, surely you'd open doors so that I could use the thoughts I am gathering about you. But everything stays closed before me like a door without a handle. You seem far away.

The urge to praise you is so strong at night I awaken with words on my lips, words that have formed within the depths of my being and want to be released.

But the people out there don't want an oldster who spent long years in another culture. They don't want my words. They don't want the truth of my phrases. They don't want a retired missionary. They want only a missionary on furlough who can tell interesting stories.

God, hear me. Show me what to do. I am in despair. I feel the bitter bile of discouragement overcoming me. I am stuck here in this congregation. I can't go back overseas, nor do I want to leave, for it was you who led the way back. Maybe if they knew the pain I feel, they could understand the need of a teacher to keep teaching and of a preacher to keep preaching, even in a limited way.

It's not that I want glory, Lord. You know I am unconcerned about praise. But my work was my life—and now I have no work. I am retired, they say. Enjoy your rest.

I would despair, O Lord, if I did not remember that you gave me this gift. The church affirmed it. The Spirit used it. I praise you for that, Lord. You are my God. I will continue to praise your name with my lips in the quietness of my room. Though I have no public voice, I can always speak to you.

Praise God from whom all blessings come.

Golden wedding

*I will sing to the Lord, I will sing; I will make
music to the Lord, the God of Israel.* (Judges 5:3)

My heart is so full, Lord, I can scarcely contain myself.
Today my husband and I celebrate fifty years together.
And it seems that only yesterday we stood at the altar and
pledged our vows to one another: "For better or for
worse, in sickness and in health, until death do us part."

People laugh at the thought of anyone spending fifty
years with the same person—too boring, too limiting, too
impossible!

But Lord, they don't know that husbands and wives
grow more beautiful to each other as they age and that
their relationship becomes richer and more comfortable.

These fifty years were all grace; I praise you for them.

During these days of celebration, my husband and I
have dug deep into the well of memory. We weren't
spared anything: severe illness, economic setbacks,
death of a son, divorce of a daughter, mortgages, gossip,
stupidity, injustice, or apathy—ours and others.

There was that terrible car accident. We moved too often in the early years. Help us forget the bitter memories. Give us grace to leave behind grudges and anger. Keep us honest with one another and with you.

Joy came with the birth of children and grandchildren, with weddings, with wonderful years of fellowship with brothers and sisters in Christ in the church. We worked with them to build the education wing and to strengthen the people of God. You ordered our steps.

I wonder how many casseroles I've carried to church. But to see young couples find peace with you and strength for the journey was worth it. As I look back, I see an amazing design in our lives which you created.

The glue that bonded us was our decision to fulfill your purposes. From the beginning we began and ended each day with a prayer of thanksgiving and request for wisdom. On our knees. We wanted to honor you.

We learned soon that to love one another means to suffer. At times our love seemed fragile, like a wisp of thread from a frayed towel, able to bear no strain. But you provided the grace to forgive and start again.

Thank you, Lord, that I had someone to stand by my side through these fifty years of sunshine and shadow, joy and pain. Thank you that I could stand beside my husband in his victories and temptations all these years. Two are always stronger than one.

Many times we clung to one another physically and emotionally in fear. We prayed not in the fullness of trust but the agony of desperation. And you understood.

On this day we cannot be silent about your great and

wonderful working in our lives. We praise your holy name. Give us courage to move into the next years with joy and a clear vision of your task for us. May our love for you and for each other grow in the years left to us.

New Year's Eve reflections

Search me, O God, and know my heart; test me and know my anxious thoughts. See if there is any offensive way in me, and lead me in the way everlasting. (Ps. 139:23-24)

Lord of all time and of all places, at the end of this year I draw near to you to praise you for the blessings of the last year.

Thank you for a warm home to shelter me and sufficient healthful food to eat.

Thank you for a sufficient measure of health and strength to meet each day with joy and anticipation of what it will bring.

Thank you for all those who have made life more comfortable for me this year—for the one who brings me the mail, for the young woman who carries my groceries to my car, for the person who catches my errors in my bank deposits.

Thank you for the choir that sings each Sunday morning and for those willing to teach the Bible lesson.

Thank you for the comfort and admonition of your Word and those who preach and teach it.

Thank you for my children and their families; thank you that they have stood the test of another year. This is only by your grace.

As I think of the year ahead, I wonder whether my remaining years will yield anything of value. I live alone. I cannot drive the car. What does the future hold?

The heavy surf that threatens the ordinary swimmer challenges the seasoned surfer to ride through it. The surf in the sea of old age is heavy at times, the waves high and tumultuous. They threaten me. Give me courage to ride through them.

As I enter the New Year, strengthen my desires to know you better. Search my heart and cleanse it from all sin. Forgive my failures. Blot out its mistakes, times of weakness, and lack of faith.

Lord God Almighty, teach me to enjoy life irrespective of how much trouble, worry, discomfort, loneliness, and misunderstanding I may face.

Give me tolerance for those who don't agree with my opinions and a readiness to change my mind when I am obviously in error.

Give me a passion for serving you and your kingdom. Show me new ways of making your name known.

And should this year be my last one, let me leave in my spiritual will the peace which Christ himself left us when he departed from this world. Amen.

IV

As another night of pain begins

Be my rock of refuge, to which I can always go;
give the command to save me, for you are my
rock and my fortress. (Ps. 71:3)

As another night of pain begins, Lord, rock of refuge,
give me courage. Help me to bear the pain which today
—and for many days—is growing worse. Give me peace
in my heart and a willingness to trust you as this night begins.

Draw close to me so that the growing darkness becomes my loving friend and warm comforter. You saw a
lot of sickness and sorrow when you lived among us. You
heard people's cries of pain. You placed your healing
hand upon those who came to you. Look upon my suffering now and heal me.

I fear the frailty of my own flesh and spirit. I cannot
understand the purpose of this pain. I want to believe in
your eternal love and wisdom, but when my body trem-

bles with the deepening pain, the long searching tentacles of uncertainty and fear reach for me. At once I am ready to raise the white flag of surrender.

I want to pray but I don't know what to ask for—a miracle of healing? The comfort of sleep? Relief from pain? The release of death? To be with you?

When I go through those gates, will they be golden? And will you be there to welcome me?

Keeper of all Israel, I thank you for your promise that you will not leave me. You have promised that nothing can separate me from your love—neither life nor death, pain nor pleasure, sadness nor joy.

You fit the burden to each person's shoulders. Your yoke is easy and the burden is light. Almighty God, Creator of all, Redeemer of all humankind and all the earth, may I hold firm to faith, aware that as I suffer you suffer with me.

Help me to bear the pain that disturbs my sleep and haunts my waking moments. Give me strength over and above my own to go through this illness. I rest in your strong arms of love. I trust in you. I can do nothing else.

My husband is ill

Cast your cares on the Lord and he will sustain you; he will never let the righteous fall. (Ps. 55:22)

O Lord my Comforter, the one to whom I have turned so often in the past, draw near to me once more.

I need you. I should be rejoicing and celebrating in your goodness this Christmas season. But instead I cry. I am anxious, much troubled.

My husband is once again not well. Slowly but surely his body is weakening.

Help us in our time of need. Heal the sick. Comfort the weary.

Four years he's been sick, and it never seems to end. His strength just slowly dwindles. When he gets an attack, I wonder whether this may be the last illness, the last time I will speak with him, hold his hand, or hear his quiet voice reach for me.

We've talked about dying. Not much, but a little. Should we be afraid? What happens at death? After? I know I should be ready to release him from his suffering, but if he dies, what then? What happens at death—to him? To me?

Will the loneliness be any worse than it is now? Life is a terribly lonely thing. We live so much apart from others when we have no regular contacts outside our home.

Visitors are few. He has been sick so long that his illness is taken for granted. People see us as coping. Yet I long for someone to lift the burden of his care from me. I am weary, Lord, very weary. And sometimes I am angry and bitter. I want to shout that life is unfair, life is too hard. So I say it to you, and I know you understand. You want to hear our cry of pain.

Yet as I rethink the last years, I recall how patient he has always been and how often he has encouraged visitors. He rarely complains, even when at his lowest. He has learned submission.

Teach me submission also, Lord. I too want to glorify your name. Let your spirit of loving compassion be my spirit as I go downstairs to heat a bowl of soup for him. You are a great God. You have helped so many in the past. You will also help me through this day.

Thank you for your love. I rest my burden at your feet. I will yet praise you for your faithfulness.

"The Lord is my light and my salvation—whom shall I fear? The Lord is the stronghold of my life—of whom shall I be afraid?"

Someone close to me has died

[Sarah] died at Kiriath Arba (that is, Hebron) in the land of Canaan, and Abraham went to mourn for Sarah and to weep over her. (Gen. 23:2)

Comforter, Sustainer. These are evil days. Like the ancient preacher said, "I have no pleasure in them."

You set the lonely in families, yet in my house—no more family. My husband is no more. My children live in another state.

The love he and I had for one another is no more. Only the darkness of sorrow and despair. I cry to you and you do not hear me. O Lord, be merciful to me and hear me in my pain.

I cannot sleep. I reach out to touch him beside me in bed—but a cold emptiness occupies his space. I make a pot of hot tea but have no one to drink it with me. I turn to tell him the news I heard about the new neighbors, but my words fall heavily to the floor.

I rise at the sound of the mourning dove to the day-long silence of my loss.

When I remember his long strides, the firm gentleness of his touch, my longing for him cuts deeply.

This box piled high with his clothes, his shoes, his ties, and his belts is ready for the thrift shop. I knew every one of his shirts, pairs of pants, jacket, handkerchiefs, and items of underwear. I knew which side of his face he shaved first, which shoe he put on last. This heap of limp clothes isn't the man who walked beside me for fifty years as best friend, lover, supporter, and comforter.

And so I weep, not for him but for myself, as I face the long nights, the longer days, and endless years. He is in a better place, never to feel again the cancer gnawing like a bull terrier at his bones.

He is seeing whom he believed. I commit him to you and to your promise that you are the resurrection and life. He that believes in you shall never die but live. Reunion day will come.

Lord God, care for me in my weariness and sorrow. And give me the rest I need this night.

Morning darkness

My God, my God, why have you forsaken me?
Why are you so far from saving me? (Ps. 22:1)

Lord, here I am before you once again. It is morning and I cannot face getting up. The heavy blanket of night still weighs me down though the sun is calling me to rise.

My body feels like a sodden mattress, heavy, droopy, and without energy. Yet the children say I have to get up each morning and eat a "decent breakfast" and go to the senior citizens' center with a cheerful spirit.

Lord, why do I have to suffer like this? Isn't it enough that I had polio as a child and nearly died? Isn't it enough that I spent weeks in bed then?

But, Lord, you gave me the persistence to keep going. I walked again. I learned to love life, even with a limp.

But now, I see that this new thing slowly controlling my body will result in even greater problems. The cane I use will be exchanged for a wheelchair, the wheelchair for a bed. And then?

Who will take care of me? Who will be concerned

about me? There is no one—no one at all. I read stories of those who praise you for your healing power, those you have restored in spirit and body so that they dance before the altar.

All these years I have tried to serve you. I have committed no gross sins. My guilt, where I have wronged someone, is open to you. Great Physician, rescue me from this daily burden of ill health—the burning in my bones, the searing pain. Release me from the fear of falling on the ice, from the paralysis caused by the cold. O God, I am afraid for the future. What shall I do? Help me!

May your great salvation, O God, protect me from distrust.

From your Holy Spirit must come my praise when I speak. Only through your Son can I praise your name. Without you I cannot see the daylight. But you have promised it will come. I thank you for the hope of tomorrow.

Nonnegotiable

I know whom I have believed, and am convinced that he is able to guard what I have entrusted to him for that day. (2 Tim. 1:12)

Hear my words, Lord. I have something to tell you. Here from my little room I call to you. I want to shout, but my heart grows faint and says, "What's the use?"

Lord, lead me to a place of greater certainty. Bring me out of this arid desert into fuller understanding of you.

Satan tempts me with the thought that my faith in you is all in my head and amounts to nothing—that Jesus is not a triumphant Savior who lives in me. Like a lost child whose mother is no where in sight, I cry to you. Draw me to you. Give me proof that you are real.

In this valley of gray monotony, I long to know you in the same way I know this table is real. I want to be touched, responded to, held. I want a deep sense of your presence, of your love, instead of this clutching at promises and finding emptiness.

All these years I have trusted you. I came to you when

lost. I praised you when joyful. I turned to you at each turning in my life. You said, "Draw near to me and I will draw near to you." Yet now my faith is tested.

I did not see your crown of thorns. I did not touch the nailprints in your hands and feet and the wound in your side. I did not see the empty tomb.

Yet you are my God, the one I trust. That is nonnegotiable. Before that even Satan must flee.

I believe the Bible is your Word of truth. All these people who translate and reinterpret the Scriptures may toss out the exact wording I memorized as a child, but they cannot take from me the spirit of truth behind the words.

I am your child, made in your holy image. As long as I have life, that life is holy and worthy of respect.

I acknowledge Christ as God incarnate and my Savior and Redeemer. Many years ago I laid my sin at Jesus' feet; I no longer feel the weight. Christ called me to follow, and I did. My experience of God springs from my faith and not my faith from my experience of you.

The Holy Spirit is the wind that pulls me toward you.

The church is your body and I, as a believer in Christ, am a member of that body, whether young and strong or old and frail; whether owner of many stocks and bonds or living from Social Security check to Social Security check; whether able to walk two miles a day or bedfast.

These are the pillars on which I rest my faith. They cannot be shaken. Lord God, begin a new work of grace in me. Put a new song in my heart. Present me faultless before the throne of God. Make me inwardly pure. Let me taste and see that you are good.

Reorientation

I will meditate on all your works and consider all your mighty deeds. (Ps. 77:12)

I cried to God for help.

I cried to God to hear me.

At night when fear seemed to swallow me, I turned to the Lord as my body turned and my mind churned and sleep wouldn't come.

I called out, "Jesus, Son of God, have mercy on me! Jesus, Son of God, have mercy on me!"

I said, "God, you seem distant. Will you never reveal your face again? Has your unfailing love disappeared with the morning mist?

"Have your promises ended this very minute?

"Have you suddenly forgotten mercy?"

I agonized.

I stormed about.

But you, Lord, kept my eyes from sleeping.
You kept them open.
You kept my mind awake.
Then I remembered you, O God, and I felt remorseful.
You are always with me.
And I had forgotten.

You brought to mind former days, other trials, other failures—but also other joys and victories.
I thought: I will appeal to the times when you gave strength,
when you made a way through the wilderness, when you forgave my sin,
when you gave me peace of mind.
I will remember your works of long ago.
I will meditate on them, yes, that's what I'll do.
Your path led through the Red Sea though your footprints were not seen.
You led your people gently, like a flock.
You, O Lord, reveal yourself in simple acts of love and deeds of kindness in human lives, not in sudden dramatic appearances with big bands, lights and loudspeakers, and boisterous fanfare.
You reveal your will through the quiet voice of your Spirit.
You show your power when your children defend truth and justice.
You show your love when your children love one another.

You show your glory when your children praise you.
You will lead me.

You will give me wisdom and show me the way. I will wait on you.

I praise your name. Hallelujah.

V

An Omega speaks

The Lord reigns, let the earth be glad; let the distant shores rejoice. (Ps. 97:1)

Today our nation is voting for new leaders. Candidates have been shouting at one another, each trying to push the other deeper into the mud. "I have truth, I have wisdom!" each proclaims.

I, an Omega, also have truth and wisdom. Hear me, all you who bow down to lesser gods.

All you who have flouted our God, tremble and quake.

The huge stockpiles of weapons the people trust in are like haystacks before our God.

When the Lord comes in his rule of righteousness and justice, all nations will glorify him.

Shame on you who worship the products your technology has produced.

Shame on you who take pride in your gleaming cars, your sleek boats, and your extravagant houses.

Bow down before the Lord, all you gods of progress and materialism.

The Lord God is our ruler.

Let the whole nation be glad.

Let all the people rejoice.

Though moral corruption and bold denial of the Lord God cloud our view of him, God is secure on his throne.

The Lord Almighty is upheld by righteousness and justice.

God's truth destroys the darkness of sin.

God's grace lifts the heaviness of despair.

God's truth releases those bound by the chains of hopelessness.

God's love brings life,

God's truth brings freedom,

God's gracious law of mercy grants holiness.

The church hears and rejoices.

Her sons and daughters lift up their voices in song at your decrees, Lord God.

For you are Lord of Lords, greater than any Great Communicator, more powerful than nuclear fission, computer chips, internal combustion engines, communications theory, and marketing strategies.

The Lord loves those who denounce evil.

He tenderly cares for those who are faithful to him.

He rescues them from the claws of the briber and the corrupter.

God-seekers do not give up,

God-lovers seek peace,

They rejoice and sing,

Peace dances in their hearts as they remember God's justice.

Praise the Lord, all you people. Today I, an Omega, vote for God's reign over us. Amen.

My own manna jar

And what does the Lord require of you? To act justly and to love mercy and to walk humbly with your God. (Micah 6:8)

Lord, I'm trembling with anger. I want to shake my fist at the world for the oceans of suffering I became aware of today.

A friend is suffering depression.

A young couple, barely married, is planning divorce.

A teenager is struggling with the divorce of her parents.

That new young mother in church gave birth to a severely handicapped child.

An older friend must cope with a new illness in addition to a long-standing disease.

The newspapers are full of stories of children dying of hunger; of refugees wandering around cold, hungry, and homeless; of assassinations and tortures.

And my friend was killed in a car accident.

Lord, make the pain stop! You've got the power! Why

don't you help if you're there and you know what is going on? Take your hands out of your pockets. Do something. You're God! You're supposed to be a good God!

Why does life have to be so hard? You let all this happen. If we're made in your image, why is that infant with severe birth defects so imperfect, so wanting? Was that your plan? Where is justice? Have you deserted your creation?

I desperately want to program faith into my soul as I do my computer. But I can't. Don't hand me over to despair. Hear me, Lord God.

I turn to you, Lover of my soul, because you alone understand my pain. I trust you. Without you I would have to face alone this puzzle of why good people suffer.

Though I long for a genie in a lamp to appear when I rub it with prayer, I trust you to do what is best. You are sovereign. You have always been faithful. This knowledge comforts me.

So here before your silence, I bring out my manna jar, even as the children of Israel turned to theirs in the temple as proof of your faithfulness.

You kept the persecuted church of Christ alive in Russia during the dreadful Stalinist years.

You raised a witness in Central America when the military forces stomped through the land destroying any voice that spoke for the oppressed.

You worked in my parents' lives, drawing them to you.

Your Spirit worked in my life, showing me the better way.

Your Spirit continues to work in my children's lives, giving them also a hunger for your truth.

This present battle with evil and violence may seem lost, but you will eventually win the war over Satan and evil.

You hold the world and the events of history in your mighty hand. One day you will bring history to a close. Even as you were in control at Creation, so you will be present and in control at the end. There will be justice one day, even though I do not understand the growing indifference to it now.

You suffered with Jesus on the cross. You too feel hurt when people suffer and violence controls the world. You agonize with those who cry out in torment.

Nothing can separate us from your love. Nothing. This manna jar proves it.

So, Lord God, I commit the violence and injustice of this world to you. I can't determine how my petitions will be answered. I come to you because you are God, sovereign Lord of all, not because you are a slot machine with blessings to dispense at the insertion of a little spiritual excitement on my part.

Show me where I, with my limited strength, can strengthen the faith of someone who is suffering; ease her burden so she can rise each morning with hope. You said that when we are most powerless, then we are strong. Give me a passion for those who suffer in body and spirit. This is my prayer.

Night song

Even though I walk through the valley of the shadow of death, I will fear no evil, for you are with me. (Ps. 23:4)

Tonight, Lord, as I sit by the window watching the shadows deepen, I think about death, the passage to another life—eternal life. I too must travel that way.

Each morning the newspaper brings news of those who died the day before. I check their ages. I pass over those who lived their allotted lifespan and then some.

But I linger over the obituaries of those who died while quite young—a fifteen-year-old in a car accident, a thirty-two-year-old with no stated cause of death. But the word is already out that it was a self-inflicted gunshot to the head. And then there's an infant who died at birth.

The spring of life is no time to die. Then young people, like plants, rush into leaf and burst into bloom.

Nor is it time to die when you are strong and healthy. Nor when the much-anticipated retirement time arrives, bringing the opportunity to set aside former activities for the challenge of a new task.

It isn't time to die even at my age. As long as I'm alive every tiny cell in my body fights to hold off the invading enemy cells. But people die at every age, and the ranks of my friends are thinning with each year.

When I think about death, I'm like a child at play who doesn't want to go to bed just yet. Playing outside in the empty lot was always most fun at the magic moment just before Mother called us in. We couldn't tear ourselves away to come in to wash up and go to bed.

I don't want to die just yet.

I want to hear the *Messiah* sung again this Christmas.

I want to see my grandson graduate from high school and my granddaughter from middle school.

I want to hold in my arms my new grandchild and watch her learn to walk.

Today I laughed at Annette's jokes until the tears ran. Tomorrow I want to laugh some more.

I want to hold my friend's hand when she returns from the chemotherapy that doesn't seem to help.

I want to tell my children again how much I love them. I never do it often enough.

And yet on the other side of the street stands a tree, bent by the wind, scarred by storms, bare of leaves. The city crew marked it with a big orange X, which means it will be cut down. It has finished living. Does it contemplate its dying? Does it fear it?

Am I afraid to die? Shall I be afraid when the time comes? It will come, I know.

At twilight, light loses and darkness wins. Yet night is

the promise of day even as death is the promise of life
and love and of the joy of your nearness, heavenly Father.

I don't want to go just yet, Lord. But when I hear you
knocking, I'll be ready, for I trust your mercy. Amen.

Eightysomething

Even to your old age and gray hairs I am he,
I am he who will sustain you.
I have made you and I will carry you:
I will sustain you and I will rescue you.
(Isa. 46:4)

Lord God Most High, Creator, Redeemer, Sustainer, I trust you. I have trusted you these many decades since I walked down the aisle of that little country church. I praise you for more than sixty years of faithfulness.

Don't let me doubt your love, especially as I age. In my silences I hear the lions of the later years growling at my door. They grow bolder, demanding entry.

I'm not sure I can keep them out. I didn't expect old age to be like this. If you don't stand by me, Lord, I won't be able to hold them back.

Hear my prayer, O Lord. For even as I face the new year, I weary of the lions of discouragement and loneliness daring me to quit trusting you.

The way ahead looks uncertain, Lord. The sand is running through an hourglass with a barrel-sized opening. Stand by me this new year. Don't let me drift through my final days like a toy boat on a fast-flowing river.

Here I am, more tired at the end of each day. Pudgy again like a kitten. Graying. Wrinkled. That snapshot the kids took showed I had jowls—hideous things. And it will just get worse. Dewlaps. Armflaps. Flaps everywhere.

Don't let me get sick. What if I fell down the stairs and broke a leg? Would anyone miss me? I could rot; who would care? This growing old is not for me, yet I can't bypass it like I can step over a mud puddle.

You've been my hope, my salvation, O God, since the youth group years ago sent me on my way with the words, "He who began a good work in you will carry it on to completion until the day of Christ Jesus."

We began together, Lord. You said I was your child. I trusted that word, Lord. I turn back to it again and again.

But when I look around I see older men and women who have subsided into mute, indifferent human beings.

I'm not thinking of those sick with Alzheimer's or something like that, but those with functioning minds and bodies. They come to church to sit. They go home to sit. The church doesn't really need them other than to fill benches, to give money, and to bring finger food.

Do not cast me away when I am old. Give me again the joy of the Lord.

Do not forsake me when my strength is gone. Though my joints ache and my grasp is weak, do not forsake me, O God, as I reach out to you. Let me again declare your glory boldly to this generation. Let me tell them the story of how you remained faithful year after year.

Though you have made me see my troubles you will restore my joy. You have done so in the past. You will do it again. I quiet my soul. Praise the Lord. Amen.

Taking communion
at home

While they were eating, Jesus took bread, gave thanks and broke it, and gave it to his disciples, saying, "Take it; this is my body." (Mark 14:22)

There are just four of us here today, Lord, meeting in your name—the pastor and his wife, the deacon and me. At first it didn't seem quite right to do it this way—on a Thursday when I've always participated in the Lord's Supper in church on a Sunday.

I long to join the others at church to eat the bread, drink the wine, hear the organ play, and sing the old hymns. But that's impossible now. I am comforted when I remember that you ate this meal with your disciples in the upper room of a home.

So this, too, is the church of Jesus Christ. We few gathered here are your body. Where one or two are gathered in your name, you're there in the midst of them.

While they were eating, Jesus took bread, gave thanks and broke it, and gave it to his disciples, saying, "Take and eat; this is my body."

Lord, you know the hunger of the human soul for a greater closeness with God, and so you gave your body, the body we partake of this Thursday afternoon.

You gave the bread a name—"my body." I eat this bread to remember I am an important member of your body. May I draw strength from knowing that I, imprisoned in this weakened body that no longer does my bidding, belong to you; your Spirit dwells in me.

Yes, I am one in the Spirit with all other believers in Christ.

I am a member of the new covenant of love.

Then he took the cup, gave thanks and offered it to them, saying, "Drink from it all of you. This is my blood of the covenant, which is poured out for many for the forgiveness of sins."

You gave this wine a name—"my blood."

I drink this wine to remember that you on the cross made alive and whole all who come to you. I stand amazed at the wonder of the one and only sufficient sacrifice.

As a young child I came to you. The cross ended the control of Satan over my life. You freed me to follow you. You made me whole.

I have this life in you because you gave it to me, and I want to let you live in me by faith in Jesus Christ.

I eat. I drink. I bless you, my Lord and Savior.

Lord, I think I am too old to pray

Even to your old age and gray hairs I am he, I am he who will sustain you. I have made you and I will carry you. (Isa. 46:4)

Rock of Ages, it came to me today. Kind of sneaked up on me. And I don't know how to say it. Lord, I think I am too old to pray.

The spirit bends less easily, the knees hardly at all.

Here I am before you, ready to pray and the words are gone—lost in my mind like my hairbrush was this morning.

"Dear Lord," I say—and then?

"Dear Lord"—I try again. "I praise your holy name"—that's how I've always begun.

For health and strength and daily food,
We praise your name, O Lord.

With four hungry children around the table and my husband at one end and me at the other, it was easy to find songs of joyful praise:

> I will praise the Lord all my life;
> I will sing praise to my God as long as I live.

But this morning, I look for the words to praise you—but my spirit is sluggish. Why not repeat what I said yesterday until my soul catches up with the day?

It's like this, God. I feel like a little child. I want to know what you have in store for me today before I say thanks. Will there be a visit from Anne, a letter from Ruth, a call from Jim?

Will my legs feel agile enough to go to the post office? Will I feel perky enough to finish knitting that afghan?

Will my eyes be clear enough to read the new book Anne brought me?

Please, God, I want to know. Faith has snail's feet today.

Always I have turned to you. You promised to be with me in time of trouble. You promised to be with me now in time of dryness of this tired spirit. My praise for you is wandering about inside this aging body, reaching for you and not finding a way out.

But you, O God, know me and understand me. Accept this emptiness of words today. Know that I love you. Here are yesterday's items of praise. Here is yesterday's list of petitions. By this evening I'll have today's ready. I know you understand. Amen.

Widow psalm

Blessed are those whose strength is in you, who have set their hearts on pilgrimage. As they pass through the Valley of Baca, they make it a place of springs. (Ps. 84:5, 6)

I will praise you, O Lord, for you have kept me in your way these many years and didn't let me fall by the wayside, even when I despaired of finding the right path.

I called to you for help during the years after my husband's death. You brought me out of the bitter darkness of sorrow.

You said it was all right to cry.

You said it was all right to be angry at those who had shoved me outside their circles.

You said it was all right to feel the pain I was enduring at the time.

Praise God, all you who mourn, for you will be comforted.

Praise our Lord's name, for his absence is not forever. Weeping may endure for a season, but joy comes with the dawn.

When my husband died, though I was sad, I felt secure. I said to myself, "God is with the widows. I will be taken care of. We'll make it—God and I. With God's strong arm underneath me, I will be able to weather the worst that can confront me." The Bible assured me of your promise.

But when you hid your face and everything went wrong, the latter darkness was deeper than the first. It was as if all my moorings had broken loose at once, casting me adrift. My former friends left me. The congregation seemed indifferent to another widow added to the growing list, another unmarried older woman to visit. Now I didn't know where to turn.

I called to you, Lord, again and again. I cried for mercy, for someone to lift the heavy burden that was bending me so low, that I couldn't drop it even during the night.

What glory was it to you if I had no joy, no strength to carry on? Does defeat praise you? Does joylessness and bitterness bless your name?

I cried for help. Don't leave me. Show me where you are. Give me some small evidence that you are with me in this mess.

You turned my sadness into gladness. I waited and found joy for the journey. You showed me that if you loved me as I was, husbandless, I could love myself. You gave me back myself. I could stand erect spiritually. I had worth in your sight. I had found the place of springs.

May my heart continue to sing your praise. I will bless your name forever, for you are my God. Amen.

Here I raise my Ebenezer

Then Samuel took a stone and set it up between Mizpah and Shen. He named it Ebenezer, saying, "Thus far has the Lord helped us." (1 Sam. 7:12)

Heavenly Father, I may not be here next year, and so I want to do what the children of Israel did after they had crossed the Jordan. They erected a monument of twelve stones to tell those passing that way what you had done for them. You stopped the flow of the river so they could cross on dry land. They wanted future generations to know that your hand was powerful and that God's people should always fear their Creator.

Here is my Ebenezer to your faithfulness and grace. I want those coming after me to know you are a great and faithful God. May my family, each one, turn to you in praise and obedience. These stones stopped the heavy flow of discouragement, bitterness, and doubt so I could cross on dry land. The stones aren't big or beautifully carved, but picked out of the jumble of daily life.

I put my first stone in place for my parents who trusted you through war, revolution, famine, and depression as Lord of all. They laid the foundation for my faith-life.

I raise my second stone for those early encouragers who saw in me someone God loved and could use in kingdom work at a time I didn't believe that myself. They sent me on my way with the promise that the One who had begun "a good work" in me would "perform it until the day of Jesus Christ."

I raise my third stone in praise of the teacher who showed compassion when I couldn't understand the lesson and gave me another chance.

I place another stone for my husband who chose me to be his life's companion and best friend. His dedication to the task of preaching the gospel never wavered from the day he first committed his life to you as a young man until his death.

I put into place a fifth stone for the friend who trusted us enough to loan us money to return to school when others said our plans were foolish. His trust gave us courage to keep your mission as our goal.

A sixth stone is for the many people who affirmed my writing with words, prayers, and kindness. They made it easier to accept myself as a worker in the kingdom.

My pile of stones is getting high. But I have more.

I place this large stone for all biographers who wrote about men and women who aimed high, invaded enemy territory with a spirit of victory, and who by sharing the story of these people's commitment to the task inspired me never to give up.

An eighth one is for my children, each one, who as they and I grew older, became my friends and kept saying, "Mother, you can do it. Keep going."

A ninth one is for those leaders, both men and women, who dared to lead the church into new thinking about the nature of the church, the body of Christ, and the priesthood of all believers.

A tenth stone is for the courageous witnesses of the gospel who, throughout the ages, have given their lives on behalf of truth. Their blood has stained the soil but given vision and strength to the church.

An eleventh stone is for older friends whom I watch carefully to find out how to walk in this untried and uncertain land of aging. They show me by their vibrancy of spirit and enthusiasm for life that the journey can be traversed with hope and joy.

Our country has a monument to the unknown soldier. I have a stone to set in place for the unknown believer who held the dike of faith despite severe trials and difficulties and kept the church of Jesus Christ alive when others deserted you.

Lord, you work through your people. They are the living stones of the church. Here I raise my Ebenezer as a tribute to your love and mercy.

> Hither by thy help I'm come.
> And I hope, by thy good pleasure,
> Safely to arrive at home. . . .
> Oh, to grace how great a debtor
> Daily I'm constrained to be!

Let that grace now, like a fetter,
Bind my wand'ring heart to thee.
(Robert Robinson, 1758)

These stones are my monument of thankfulness to
you for your working in my life these many decades.
Lord, I have kept the faith. All that is necessary has been
accomplished. Amen.